More Praise for Story & Bone

Story & Bone is deeply connected to the flora and fauna of the poet's native Brazil, her adopted New England, and many geographies in between. Its poems shed light on the experience of joy in the blazing colors of the rainforest as well as the unmistakable palette of the northern spring. And the poems explore collective and personal histories: we learn family accounts of leaving one world for another, crossing borders as refugees. We see the perilous moment of the poet's own birth, the umbilical cord around her neck, and the perilous birth of her twin daughters who, in later poems, are thriving, holding "the light, the dark of my countries." The collection asks what home is and provides an answer: home is what we weave through the music and pattern of language and through the life we live with others, season by season, year by year.
— **Jennifer Barber**, author of *The Sliding Boat Our Bodies Make*

"The very first poem of Deborah Leipziger's gorgeous new collection recalls "my mother told me no one/would ever love me/like she did. Now I know/ she was right and wrong." Leipziger is the poet of paradox, both its sharp edges and its soft wonder: "I channel the coincidental/the purely purposeful." Her poems are equally "untamed/like the undiscovered species creeping through the mangrove/on silent paws of night" and "this school girl immersing in jonquils./ No, those are my daughters amidst the blooms." She will "sink stanzas into your marrow/and sonnets into the lesions," placing "tercets inside the wounds" Even the order of the poems understands that "Trees know not to crowd one another./ Nature thrives in intervals,/in the intercession." With each poem read, I said to myself, "Surely, it can get no better than this?" Then I turned the page: I was right and wrong."
— **Wayne-Daniel Berard**, author of *Art of Enlightenment* and founding co-editor, *Soul Lit*

In Deborah Leipziger's new book of poetry, I have the distinct impression of the poet as an earth mother. Her poems are fecund, fertile; her body is easily integrated into the flora and the fauna. She seems to walk like Whitman, taking in the world, embracing everything, wearing them like talismans draping on her flowing dress.
— **Doug Holder**, Co-President of the New England Poetry Club

"The most wonderful thing about Deborah Leipziger's poetry is that it leaves one feeling happy to be alive. For the life described in Leipziger's work is always deeply connected to the beauty and mystery of the world outside of herself, to its bounty: flowers, trees, sex, love, oceans, skies, people, and food. She makes it all come alive so vividly that we experience it all with her—and are deeply grateful that she brought us along."
— **Lawrence Kessenich**, Author, Poet, Playwright, Winner of the Strokestown International Poetry Prize in Ireland

The poems in Deborah Leipziger's *Story & Bone* are centered around connection, the forging of it, the strength of it and the loss of it. She writes of the connections between mother and daughter and between the daughter and her own three daughters. She writes of the broken and whole sensual and emotional connections between lovers and partners. She explores her connection with nature [especially flowers], with Judaism, with her body, her past, her intentions. This leads to strong, quirky and intelligent poems.
— **Marge Piercy**, Author, Novelist, Poet, Activist, and Feminist icon

Deborah Leipziger's poems light fires! Her poetry is deeply personal, full of sensual love and of life. She cares deeply and because of her caring, we care. *Story & Bone* contains a deep affection for people, flowers, plants and defenders of nature. In a world that is often cruel, she brings excitement, joy and happiness. Leipziger is a poet to admire and enjoy.
— **Zvi A. Sesling**, editor, *Muddy River Poetry Review*

"Deborah Leipziger's *Story & Bone* dives deep into language in search of identity, memory, intimacy, and connection. But whatever they seek, these poems never forget that our yearnings are contained and enriched by our blunt bodies, with our hands stained by garden dirt, birth blood, and baking flour. They are sensual telegrams to the soul."
— **Adam Sol**, author, *The Way a Poem Moves*

Story & Bone

Deborah Leipziger

LILY POETRY REVIEW BOOKS

Library of Congress Control Number: 2022948842

Cover design and Layout: Michael d'Entremont McInnis

ISBN: 978-1-957755-10-6

Published by Lily Poetry Review Books
223 Winter Street
Whitman, MA 02382
https://lilypoetryreview.blog/

This book is dedicated to my muses: my partner Andy Hoffman and my daughters, Natasha, Allie and Jackie, and with gratitude for my wonderful parents, Fabia Terni and Michael Leipziger.

Contents

I

Sugaring   3
What is home   4
Self, Archaeologist   5
Written on Skin   8
Inheritance   9
Finding the Mother Tree – A Cento   10
Radiation on Valentine's Day   11

II

The body has always been a writing   13
Blue Fugue   14
Snowclocks   15
Lemonade   16
Daffodil Waves   17
Apple Orchard   18
How to Make Challah   19

III

To S   22
Flower Map   23
Island Cities   24
Sueño   25
Monday morning, San Juan   26
The Northern Lights   27
Self Portrait   28
Wild Calla   29
Pomegranate   30
Let it be unspoken   31

Breaking up on the Corner of 36th and 8th   32

Flower Skulls   33

In the main reading room   34

What my body remembers   35

On Plum Island   36

Brimming   37

Ode to Hand Washing   38

The way the iris opens   39

Gates of the Beloved   40

IV

After the bombing they quoted Emily Dickinson   42

Venom   43

Vessel   44

Sugaring II   45

By the bay, before the breakup   47

To the person who wrote to the Dictionary to ask how
    long love lasts   48

V

The Creation of Turquoise   50

Lobo   51

You as a forest   53

The shyness of crowns   54

Vigil   55

Darwin's Questions   56

How to help a friend mourn   57

Altar   59

Story & Bone

I

Sugaring

After Safia Elhillo

i was made of almonds and sugar
of giving and receiving
coast lines dug deep   with departure
of boats and boundaries   seeking refuge

for my Nonna, all desserts   began
with recreating home
in a latticework of
marzipan

i was born under dictatorship   under the light
of the southern cross
dissolving into coconut   and clove   tangled
in the umbilical cord

my mother told me   no one
would ever love me
like she did.   now I know
she was right   and wrong

my daughters born of gingerbread
under a coup d'ivorce
hold the light, the dark
of my countries

What is home

a house made of kites
and orchids bleeding
is home.

language and story
color is home.

home is story   memory
and the bones I carry

a library where
books
bleed into each other
green valleys
cobalt feathers
golden letters on their spines.

I want
to let the stories pour into me.

I did not know that everything
would be taken away.

Only later did I learn that
my Grandparents sewed gems
into the hems of their clothing
for each border crossing.

Self, Archaeologist

After Walt Whitman

I celebrate myself and sing myself
my colors and countries
symmetries and symbols
the color of veins
reddening purple,
my pulsating heart

I sing the temples   beloved
the words   recovered
the mazes   discovered

I celebrate my nimbus of curls
nipples   neck   navel

I celebrate my survival
from the umbilical cord
wrapped around my neck

I celebrate my geography
canyons   mesas
my Amazon   my Nile.

The planets whisper to me,
constellations call me
chanting of Newness

I open myself and claim my
openness
I transform and sing
my Evolution

I celebrate the concave
and convex
the rounded   the bonded
the turning   becoming
the rawness   evolved
I sing the poets before me
pollinating my poems
I sing of the borders
my ancestors crossed
gems sewn in hems

Or is it legend?
I celebrate the fiction and non-fiction
the manic and tragic
festivals past   holidays not
yet named
I honor and celebrate the Becoming

I channel the coincidental
the purely purposeful
the rant   the chant
the prayer   the poem

I rejoice in sleep
swallowing the tidal grief,
the delirium

I sing the mycelium
the chariots   the twilight
the self
The castle   fort   water tower
lighthouse   reservoir
all built within me

I mourn the forests
turned to desert   the polar caps
to water

I believe in the ancestors
joining me   a happy ghosting,
I escaped for you
I am because you are

I approach the wild
the chameleons
changing blue to green
red to yellow and back.

I am the bromeliad
collecting water
aromatic   the lilac

I honor my departures
all the places
where I emerge
Welcomed
Complete

Written on Skin

In cursive script your kiss
licked indelibly on skin.

The umbilical cord coiled
around my neck, pulsates on skin.

The forest willow for the violin
music etched on wood, on skin.

The scar from my twins' birth
echoes the rain, written on skin.

Numbers from Auschwitz
blast-furnaced on skin.

The parchment of history of sacrifice
branded on hides, stories on skin.

Buildings collapse
in Bangladesh, grafted on skin.

Gems faceted by stone
hidden in garments, etched on skin.

Your touch on my earlobe, fingerprints on my face
Deborah written on skin.

Inheritance

Where do you end and I begin?
I once lived in your body,
your blood   in my veins.

Your grief grafted onto me,
I carry your sadness
like lichen
growing over itself in layers
into the cavities   of the tree   its lacerations
etching maps of ancient forests
in the trees
until your pain is mine.

You gift me your grief   filigree
and interlaced parts   design by perforation.
Transcribed in hieroglyphics,
I am caught   in your spirograph.

Pain has its own beauty   a patina of verdigris.
The birch trees with its eyes   covered in snow.
The false eyes   of fish and butterflies

Nature washes wounds,
as salt forms a delicate crust   on the waves
of melancholy rage.

Your gift to me.

Finding the Mother Tree – A Cento

She was the fire I didn't know,
Beautifully, impossibly, unspeakably wild

The tongue of the river
Rising and growing bigger

The ancestors want to wash
And said I'm sorry, sorry, sorry.

Radiation on Valentine's Day

For Janice Silverman Rebibo

I want to radiate your cells with poetry
to sink stanzas into your marrow
and sonnets into your lesions.
I want to place tercets inside your wounds
dress the cavities and densities,
let the words coil into your clavicle
until the sestinas nest
tibia and tendon
until
bone by bone
You are returned.
Let the verse in,
vertebrae by vertebrae
rose by rose
vein by vein

II

The body has always been a writing

With lines from Cecilia Vicuna

a calligraphy
of arteries and veins
of tributaries and pools,
platelets and cells which
travel
across looms, across time.
Cellular
threadiness,
umbilical umbra
weave into the placenta
& threshold
that connect me to you.

The line
from twin to twin
born
too early
from linen
and limb.
The mother womb
that untethered
daughters,
my sun, my moon.

Blue Fugue

When you were born, the Room turned Blue.
I became Blue   cold   veins   frozen.
The Blue became a Room.

Both of you Blue whisked away.
I, cut open.
When you were born, the Room turned Blue.

In a Blue gown,
My mouth unable to form ice words.
The Blue became a Room.

When I was born, I was Blue.
The womb was Blue the Blue cord around my neck.
When you were born the Room turned Blue.

Alone waiting warming,
Until they brought you back.
The Blue Sky becomes a Room.

Snowclocks

The lingering night
reveals snowdrops.

I squint
to see bulbs
splitting
underground.

In the lives of mothers
there is an invisibility,
a lingering night.

So, with snowdrops,
huddled, against the dark
tree trunks, an x-ray.

My life measured
not in days or hours
but in the cycle of flowers,
crocus to daffodil
tulip to peony.

Lemonade

Honeysuckle poised to open yellow
Sunflowers just a clover tall
Lazy dandelion wishes.

Yellow or pink?
Both.
Ice, plastic tumblers, a heavy jug.
You are the Maker, Mama.

Under protective trees,
my daughters await their first pouring.

Daffodil Waves

I.
"The *colline* were covered in daffodils,"
my Nonna tells me.

II.
Green grows yellow
with swollen seeds.
How suddenly they open
releasing their egg yolk trumpets.

III.
How quickly change arrives unbidden.

IV.

I am this school girl immersing in jonquils.
No, those are my daughters amidst the blooms.

Apple Orchard

We ladder up into the crown
beholden to rain and light
for apples
their purple dust,
splattering of stars

This longing to cradle
my twin daughters
as when they scampered
limbs and branches

Heart to heart, the Cortlands grow
as doubles. The sign says: "Use both hands
to pick both apples, at the same time"

The apples in my open palms
this tugging of heart, this twisting apart

How to Make Challah

Begin with the biggest bowl you have,
large enough to contain your whole week.
You'll need to wrestle with angels.

Begin in the place of knowing,
the place that venerates.
Kavannah.

In the smallest nesting bowl,
proof the yeast in lukewarm water.
Remember that you are proof.

Let the yeast envelop you,
rain, wet earth, fecund.
Trust.

Measure 7 or 8 cups of flour,
challah is not precise.
Notice the flour cloud.

Make a well.
A deep well to contain the grief.
Pour the yeast water into the well.

Let it seep.
Add 3 eggs and 3 tablespoons of oil.
Take off your rings.

Plunge.
Pound.
Rage.

Pour yourself into the challah,
filament and fractal
fingertip and phial.

Give it a few hours to grow.
Let the growth surprise you.
Add raisins, golden and black.

Set a tiny marble of dough,
apart, to recall loss, braid
as if this is your last act.

After the braids have doubled in size,
entrust them to the oven
under a coat of egg wash.

Let the aroma
permeate your village
with rest and kindness.

Bring forth the challah with both hands.

III

To S

Draw me a map of your body,
your tender places of longing.

Guide me through
your Atacama desert.

Take me through
the disbelief,
the fingerprints
that caused you pain

Guide me through the caves
into the canyons.

Let us enter the caldera
and traverse this
newly created
earth.

Flower Map

The flamboyant tree is my sign:
turn towards the path
hidden by jasmine.

A black bird accompanies me
past fronds
and thorns
the gates a mosaic of longing.

Peeling
layers of green maroon bark.
Yes, this is the path.

Are those frangipani falling
onto the sidewalk
a core of yellow? Magenta

bougainvillea
spill over the roof.
I am lush and wild in my joy.

Island Cities

Silence between us, eloquent and fluid,
a river between two cities.

The night washes
amber over our cities.

Over the hollow
we venture from petrified cities.

Story and bone
lost through forgotten cities.

How many stars,
my giver of stars, between our cities?

The jasmine scent
quivers inside our cities.

Miles and mines call us
in the path between our cities.

Sueño

I sleep inside your sleep
Your touch in my touch
Your hand resting on the
Guitar curve of my body

Thigh by thigh
The moon reclining into night
Your sweat in my pores

I dream inside your dream
Awake into our morning

Monday morning, San Juan

I drink coffee
from beans you grind
strong, dark, bubbled with creamy
milk you froth

The smell of toast
reaches for us
as we eat slices of pineapple
and papaya

The hummingbirds cannot resist

The Northern Lights

Green and pulsating like a heartbeat you tell me

We had gone out
heeding the call:
go out into that good night

Sometimes purple yellow bruise

Green growing paler

Afterglow of thunder

Memory is a painter

Self Portrait

Guava
the calyx of pomegranate
like a river

Add the white pigment
sea foam   moonlight

Black ink for my hair and eyes
black as the words on a map
calligraphy lashes

Childhood fair
colors on a spinning wheel
blurring

Wild Calla

The calla offers up its spadix
a spike   a yellow torch
suspends the inflorescence.

A spath surrounds the spadix
a flame,
a billowing white gown.

Emerging from one rhizome
one wild calla
connects all callas
buried in an underworld,

brings me to
the edge
of the water
to witness
the wild

Pomegranate

my planet in cross section
translucent and dense
a collision between vermillion and rose
completeness
a thing unto itself
prehistoric, biblical
an evolution
enclosed

Let it be unspoken

This current
from broken to whole

Unbound
a spool never quite wound again

Let it be untamed
like the undiscovered species
creeping through the mangrove
silent on the paws of night

Breaking up on the Corner of 36th and 8th

Your wall-size canvas
a charcoal tree against a blue sky
A girl suspended in the air

A gelato of passion fruit
its ice a flower of petals
fragola, limoncello, lampone

Sitting on a stranger's stoop
after my wallet is stolen
sucking in big gulps of air

Touching fingers at the movie
in the Village
the last row

Washington Square at night
illuminated by a mandala of glitter and chalk,
the sound of the fountain

The way you scan my eyes for tears
your fingers in my hair

Flower Skulls

for Georgia O'Keefe

In the clouded desert
flowers become skulls

the poppy you see
so black at its leafy core

The white iris
has tongues
of the palest pink
and yellow flares
with green echoes.

And the red canna
of pale lavender plumes
as its core.

A half truth
to say I painted flowers.

The yellow cactus flowers,
now they are a pair
side by side
overshadowed, blooming
in waves.

In the main reading room

I

My earring falls to the marble floor
The sound echoes
Mother of pearl.

II

I watch you circumnavigate the room
paying homage to the books and sculptures,
Science holds her globe and Art her paint brush & palette.

III

Your hand lingers on my back
as if there are notes to be played

the pod from the tree curves
so full of seeds.

What music are you tapping on my back?

What my body remembers

Throughout the night
the blinds create patterns
on our naked skin.
Black and white bands of light
and darkness.
Your torso over mine bathed in chiaroscuro.

On Plum Island

From my fingers
you taste the dark plum
its yellow and red interior.

The sun is poised to set
as the birds return,
egrets and gulls
to the marsh.

The pale lavender ocean

Brimming

I am filled with you
your incantations
our longitudes and latitudes

your
aurora borealis
green
across night sky

your E.E. Cummings
and my Neruda,
yes   yes   yes

bridges we crossed
like blue-lit bones

the grasshopper in my house
on the summer night you arrived

The moaning moon bathing

I am filled with you

Ode to Hand Washing

Honeysuckle, verbena
scent of lily
friction of palms floral
anoints the fingers

Rinsing,
lingering,
steeples baptized
hands open
this long-awaited lifting of all
that became contaminated.
The concentrate of day,
of summer.
this balm,
this distillation of time
the sacred
ending the day.
My ritual ablution.

Like the hummingbird
entering the flower
the scent of honeysuckle
becomes part of my journey.
I hold my own hand.

The way the iris opens

Ventricle by ventricle,
releasing
an internal map

a propulsion from within
emerging
lavender and plum

The way the iris closes
is a reversal,
a folding in

like a scroll
of parchment,

gathering its edges until
its veins visible
it becomes itself.

Gates of the Beloved

"The gates made of light swing open.
You see in."
— Rumi

Your blue eyes beckon
me to enter your city
Ancient   lovely   petrified.

I enter with offerings –
Pomegranates and honey dates.
All that I will be is here.
Entering.

IV

After the bombing they quoted Emily Dickinson

A penumbra punctures the silence
sirens
the phone.
The helicopters hovered for days.

We are OK we tell friends from Brazil and Nigeria.

My eyes meet strangers' eyes
bearing our city
in lockdown
contained and seething.

Life could not really continue as before
though the cherry blossoms have opened
and the seventy year old dogwood
flowers outside my window

Venom

My mouth holds venom.
How the last consonant
longs to drip
from my mouth

Just as the snake can be milked,
take the venom from my fangs
each pearl drop

Take it –
its antidote in your mouth

Vessel

Jerusalem leads me
to iridescent glass vases
the darkest purple
waning blues
greens so pale
it seems the Dead Sea pours forth.

The colors bleed
remembrance
shifting.
Collecting.

Sugaring II

The sap is rising in the trees
my bucket gathers clear sap
dripping, filling, slowly sweet
dark winter in a silent wood
waiting, waiting now for spring
the tree shivers when it's cold.

The trees shiver in the cold
the sap is rising in the trees
a trickle from the trunk will spring.
Each hour collects more sap
maples releasing in the dark wood.
It is the cold that makes it sweet.

Sap rising, falling, thick and sweet
the tree is giving in the cold.
So many taps to place in the wood
from the crown of the tree
to the gash it will flow, this sap.
Slowly, slowly comes the spring.

The nightdreams overflow with sap
with the secret longing of the wood.
How many nights of aching cold
before the forsythia of spring?
Crystals of ice, crystals of sweet.
The sap is falling in the trees.

On this cold night, does it hurt the tree?
Blood sap sweet
in the wood, from veins spring.

By the bay, before the breakup

"It's abalone," you say
fingering the shell that hangs
around my neck.

Your eyes take in my every pore
my eyes
my lashes

The tiny grooves along
the edge,
a row of apertures
that gives me away.

This which once breathed
lies in your palm,
nacreous contours radiate

Now alone
I caress
this small ear of the ocean.

To the person who wrote to the Dictionary to ask how long love lasts

Love closes
forecloses
rearranges itself
like a window display.

It goes underground,
for years perhaps,
to hibernate
until it is called forth,
It can rest on wings
and die suddenly on a January night.

Love lives in words
and deeds.
Can be uncovered
Rewound
Recycled
Revisited, rejoined
Reneged.

No one,
not even the lexicographers, know
how long it lasts.

V

The Creation of Turquoise

It didn't happen all at once
the elders would say.
Then it seldom does.

It was the inexorable
chipping away of the sky
one kernel at a time.

When the sky touched the earth
the impact created
turquoise
to tell the story
of sky and earth colliding

Lobo

For Paulo Paulino Guajajara, an indigenous leader known as "Lobo", who was a
"Guardian of the Amazon", killed by illegal loggers

I guard the forest
its canopy of reflected stars
the morpho butterflies   the blue moons
bromeliads   the fish
the roots of trees
   drinking in the river

I guard the forest
the children of the tribe

I guard the canopy with its toucans   parakeets
emerald
I guard the forest floor   with its snakes
I guard the mating jaguars

I knew
they would kill me.
I could not have imagined
that it would be a shot to the
face   that my body would be
left in the forest

Now
You guard the forest
its canopy of reflected stars
the morpho butterflies   the blue moons

bromeliads   the fish
the roots of trees
    drinking in the river

You guard the forest
the children of the tribe

You guard the canopy with its toucans   parakeets
emerald
You guard the forest floor   with its snakes
You guard the mating jaguars

You as a forest

I listen to the shelter of you
the sweeping canopy cradling the day
and night of me
the moon rising in your branches
the stars falling into the sweep of your hair.
I see the feet of your forest
the fingers, the limbs
the concave and convex of you,
the light that falls around us.
I smell your maple,
fern, ivy.

The light serpentine
falling through the rings
of redwoods

The shyness of crowns

The canopies of trees
hold shyness.

Trees know not to crowd one
another.

Nature thrives in intervals,
in the intercession.

Vigil

for the Ukraine

The open window, the birds, the rain,
all stand sentry.

May they linger.

Darwin's Questions

Upon reading Oliver Sacks, The River of Consciousness

We evolve together
in the way of orchids
and pollinators –
Bats bees moths,
hummingbirds
in the dance
of co-evolution.
         Moths
appear, at night.
The orchid's pollinia–
a circle of pollen —
seeks
a certain pollinator.
On the Isle of Reunion
the bee orchid lures male
bees.
      The orchid's iridescent
      wing
resembles the female bee,
      creating allomones,
      which mimic the scent
      of female bees.
The hawkmoth,
reaches into the white
star
of the orchid.

How to help a friend mourn

After Ellen Bass

For this you will need lemons.
Plant a lemon tree.
Grow it in an arid place.

Maybe you won't have time to grow a lemon tree,
but you have planned for this moment,
this is why you've grown a lemon tree.

Grate the lemons, collecting their juice,
perfuming your fingers,
zest until all that is left is the hollowed sun.

Gather blueberries as you did
with your daughters.
You remember – early in the morning,

Before the heat,
running wild
blueberries through your fingers.

Soften the butter-brick.
Remember that baking is coaxing.
Sugar the butter into snow.

Add the lemon juice   zest   vanilla.
Notice the flour is nearly finished. Feel the gratitude
for the second
bag wedged deep in the pantry.

Add eggs   one by one   and watch them
dissolve into the snow.
Remember the almond flour.
Grief is gritty.

Forgive yourself the small transgression,
the little vanilla pond on the counter.

Remember, healing needs tending.
So much depends on Listening.

Ottolenghi calls for a glaze
but the cake is best bare,
with its blueberry veins exposed.

Carry the warm cake to your friend's house
covered with a tea towel.
Let the light envelop her.

Altar

Begin with stillness. Summon
Courage. *Kavannah*.
Deliverance.
Essence. A beginning.
Forsythia and purple iris, tulips so pink   edge into blue.
Gather your dearest, the lonely within and without. Bring your
Hunger, your fast.
Indeed, there is so much to hold here, to heal.
Just about everything calls out to you to be done and you must choose
Kindness, stay kind.
Love
Mystery, Mastery. All this is
Necessary.
Open to the sacred, the simple.
Pass over trifling annoyances, Make room for
Quiet places.
Reveal the past.
Sacrifice the things that no longer serve you. Remember the
Temples burning in Paris, in Jerusalem, in yourself. Listen, the
Universe calls to you.
Verify, purify.
Wake up your ancestors around the table.
Yearn for justice and freedom, bring your
Zeal. Bring your self, your deep desire to connect
    the past, the possible, time no longer linear

Notes

P. 7 – *What is Home*
Written at the Institute of Contemporary Art, Exhibit "When home won't let you stay," 2019.

P. 8 – *Written on Skin*
The phrase "Written on Skin" is the title of an opera by George Benjamin.

P. 11 – *Finding the Mother Tree – A Cento*
Sources:
Ferris, Jabr, "The Secret Life of Trees," *New York Times Magazine*, December 6, 2020
Edward Hirsch, *Stranger by Night* p. 4
Terry Tempest Williams, *Erosion* p 29
Terry Tempest Williams p. 9
Marie Howe, *What the Living Do*, p 52
Rachel Kann, *How to Bless the New Moon*, p. 23
Carol Ann Duffy, *Selected Poems*, p. 41

P. 15 – *The body has always been a writing*

The lines in italics are drawn from Cecilia Vicuna's poem "With a Little Notebook at the Met".

Acknowledgments

Thank you to the brilliant and kind Eileen Cleary and the team at Lily Poetry Review Books for this journey and the book you hold in your hands.

Thank you to my partner, the amazing author, Andy Hoffman, who is both my muse and advisor.

Thank you to my poet mentors and teachers: Afaa Michael Weaver, Janice Silverman Rebibo, Marie Howe, Marge Piercy, Ellen Bass, Rachel Kann, Joan Houlihan, Carolyn Zaikowski, Jennifer Barber, Danielle Georges, Zvi A. Sesling, Gloria Mindock, Doug Holder, Kathleen Spivack, Wayne-Daniel Berard, Jeffrey Perkins, Doug Holder, Padraig O'Tuama, Tina Cane, Tzynya L. Pinchback, and Robbie Gamble.

Thank you to teachers who offered workshops in museums: Martha Collins at the Institute of Contemporary Art and Krysten Hill at the Museum of Fine Arts.

Thank you to members of my various writers group, including: Ruth Chad, Lawrence Kessenich, Grace Massey, Megan Scudellari, Mark Elber, Susan de Sola, and Janet Banks.

Thank you to the wonderful poets and writers who have provided encouragement and advice along the way: Rhina P. Espaillat, B. Lorraine Smith, Heather Wishik, and Jill Perlman.

Thank you to the T. S. Eliot House where I did some of the final edits and review of the manuscript.

Thank you to my teacher, Dona Emma, in São Paulo, Brazil who first gave me poetry assignments.

Many thanks to the editors of the following publications in which some of these poems, or earlier versions, originally appeared:
Amethyst Review: "The way the iris opens," "Holding Open," "Darwin's Questions," "Vigil"

Constellations, "What is Home"
First Literary Review - East, "On Plum Island", "Island Cities"
Ibbetson Review: "Ode to Handwashing"
Lily Poetry Review: "Sugaring", "Vigil"
The Lyrical, Somerville Times: "Daffodil Waves," "The Northern Lights are Fading"
The Mom Egg Review: "What my body remembers"
Muddy River Poetry Review: "Written on Skin," "On Plum Island," "Abalone," "Vessel," "Venom," "Brimming," "The Creation of Turquoise" "Apple Orchard", "You as a forest", "*The body has always been a writing*", "To the person who wrote to the dictionary to ask how long love lasts"
Nixes Mate Review: "The shyness of crowns"
Pangyrus: "Lobo"
Pensive: "Altar"
POESY: "Radiation on Valentine's Day"
Poetic Mindset: "How to Make Challah"
Revista Cardenal: "Lobo", "You as a forest", and "The Creation of Turquoise"
Salamander: "Daffodil Waves"
San Pedro River Poetry Review, "How to help a friend mourn"
Scribblers on the Roof: "How to Make Challah"
Soul-Lit: "Flower Map," "To S," "Sueno," "Sugaring II," "Island Cities," "Portrait," "How to Make Challah," "Poemgranate"
Wilderness House Literary Review: "What my body remembers"

Anthologies

Tree Lines: 21st Century American Poems: Greyson Press, 2022, "Lobo"
Bagels with the Bards Anthology #5: "To S"
Bagels with the Bards Anthology #6: "Everywhere around me"
Bagels with the Bards Anthology #7: "On the Corner of 36th and 8th"
Bagels with the Bards Anthology #9: "Flower Skulls"
Bagels with the Bards Anthology #10: "Radiation on Valentine's Day"
Bagels with the Bards Anthology #11: "In the main reading room"
Bresler, Ken. *Poetry Made Visible*, "In the main reading room", 2017

Chapbook: *Flower Map*, Finishing Line Press 2013: "Flower Map,"
"Island Cities," "To S," "Sueno," "Monday morning in San Juan," "The
Northern Lights are Fading," "Portrait," "The Creation of Turquoise,"
"Pomegranate," "Let it be unspoken," "On the Corner of 36th and 8th,"
"Snowclocks," "Lemonade," "How to Make Challah".

About the Author

Deborah Leipziger is a poet, author, and advisor on sustainability. Deborah's poems have been published in the UK, the US, Canada, Mexico, Colombia, Israel, and the Netherlands, in such magazines and journals as *Pangyrus, Salamander, Lily Poetry Review,* and *Revista Cardenal.* Four of her poems have been nominated for a Pushcart Prize. She is the co-founder of Soul-Lit, an on-line poetry magazine which features spiritual poetry. Her chapbook, *Flower Map,* was published by Finishing Line Press (2013). Born in Brazil, Deborah is the author of several non-fiction books on sustainability and human rights issues. She advises companies and organizations around the world on sustainability and human rights issues. Deborah co-founded the New England Jewish Poetry Festival and is the mother of three daughters, her muses.